SOUL GROWING II

Wisdom for 13 year old girls from women around the world

Collected & Edited by Quanita Roberson

SOUL GROWING

WISDOM FOR 13 YEAR OLD GIRLS FROM
WOMEN AROUND THE WORLD

Collected & Edited by Quanita Roberson

AKAN
PUBLISHING

4515 Allison Street, Suite 12412
Cincinnati, Ohio 45212-9998

Email: info@akanpublishing.com
www.akanpublishing.com

Executive Editor: Quanita Roberson

Illustration & Book Design: Elizabeth H. Murphy
www.illusionstudios.net

ISBN: 979-8-9892322-5-3 (Paperback)
ISBN: 979-8-9892322-3-9 (ebook)
Library of Congress Control Number: 2018937267

Published by Akan Publishing

This book is dedicated to my daughter, Makayla. Being your mom has taught me so much about what it means to be a deep hearted, lifelong learner, who is creative, smart, funny, and soulful. I can't wait to see more of who you will be in the world. You remind me to show up and be really present in everything I do. I want to be just like you when I grow up. I love you more.

This book is also dedicated to the 13 year old girl in me and in all the women who have been a part of my life, my teachers, my mothers and grandmothers, my aunties and sisters, my friends and clients, and my community daughters. I have learned how to love more because of who you are in the world. You have loved me into being. I love you more and more everyday.

TABLE OF CONTENTS

INTRODUCTION – ABOUT THE AUTHORS

The women in this book are all women who I know. They are women from various parts of my life, some knew me as a kid, others I met as a young adult or in my mid-life. I feel enriched by
their presence. These women were born and raised in the United States, Germany, South Africa, India, Brazil, Canada, Mexico, Australia, Denmark, Austria, and Japan. They range from their teens to their eighties. They represent different religious experiences and different sexual orientations. They are strong and soft, smart and funny, brave and loving. They are a beautiful
and powerful presence in the world. You make me proud to be a woman.

YOU ARE A PART OF EVERYTHING

"Paradise has never been about places. It exists in moments. In connection. In flashes across time."

-Victoria Erickson

CHENE SWART

PRETORIA, SOUTH AFRICA

When I was 13 I wish someone would have told me that I am not alone or mad and that there is a wonderful community that will dare to dream and journey with me into a world beyond what I could ever imagine.

LORRAINE TILBURY

PERNAY, CENTRE, FRANCE

If someone had told me when I was 13 that I could trust my intuition and inner voice in any situation, as guidance for what to do next, I would have a very different life experience today.

KELLY MCGOWAN

NEW YORK, NEW YORK

As a teen it's your job to question everything. Don't be fooled into believing there is an answer.

TONALEA JONES

My place in the world is much bigger than what I see everyday.

RENUKA TANEJA

DELHI, INDIA

I wish someone would have told me more about life when I was 13, I would have understood the world and may have been able to handle life better

ART MATTERS

"Art is the only thing big enough to contain fear and anger.
When you think terror is the biggest thing know that art is bigger."

-Fanchon Shur

SARAH CORBETT

ST. LOUIS, MISSOURI

When I was 13 I wish someone had told me.... Don't put your parents on a pedestal. They will make mistakes, they will sometimes disappoint you. That is okay. They are only human and they are who they are as a result of their childhood which was difficult in ways you cannot understand. They are always doing the best they can. The most important thing is they love you deeply, with all of their hearts. Don't try to change them. Love them for exactly who they are. Focus instead on learning how to express yourself and build your confidence. One great way to do this is by creating art of any kind... keeping some of your creations for yourself and giving some to loved ones.

CHRISTINA BALDWIN

WHIDBEY ISLAND, WA

When I was 13 I wish someone would have told me that the confusing, self-doubting, big-dreaming voice in my head was my life story trying to get itself organized. I wish they would have showed me how writing in a journal could make sense out of nonsense. (Who showed me this was Anne Frank and reading her diary in 8th grade English class. Her inspiration is with me still: a girl has a voice—and so can you have a voice.)

REGINA M. SEWELL

ORANGE, CALIFORNIA

I wish someone would have told me at 13 that it was o.k. for me to cry. That it was o.k. for me to be sensitive. It was o.k. for me to feel exactly what I felt because those feelings made me human and they made me a young adult. They allowed me to connect with other people at a richer, deeper level. It allowed me to express myself in my songs. To connect with people that way. Through feelings, through emotions. I wish someone would have said to me at 13, "you know the reason why you express and want to express in songs is because you *do* feel and you are sensitive. It serves you best to engage with that feeling in those songs." I wish someone would have said to me, "let's explore those emotions and feelings together. I love what you've written. I love that you explore your own emotions from the highs to the lows. I love how excited and passionate you are about life and how you can turn a dull room into laughter and at the same time experience the depths of pain and sorrow and express it in ways that maybe some of us older than you cannot. It's a gift, it's an art and it's something you have that you do very well. It's natural for you and whatever I can do to support you to be creative, to continue to write, to continue to sing, to continue to express it in that way, I'm in your corner. I got you. Even when I'm not here, know that you got it and that it's a gift, an asset. It's something for you to use; don't lose sight of that. And don't let anyone tell you that it's a weakness or vulnerability. It's your strength. Feeling deeply and sensitivity are your greatest strength. Be it, use it and be strong and courageous in it and not afraid of what others may say about it. It is a gift.

JOANNA POWELL COLBERT
LUMMI ISLAND, WASHINGTON

When I was 13, I wish someone would have told me to trust my instincts and not be swayed by others. I wish they'd told me I didn't need male approval to prove my worth. I wish someone had told me to be more rebellious and not bottle up everything inside. That making mistakes is not the end of the world, and gaining experience is all about trial and error. I wish they'd told me that a connection to nature is my birthright and art heals. I wish someone had told me that I would grow up to be a strong woman with a powerful voice, who really could and would make a living from the creative arts. That there was nothing I couldn't do if I set my mind to it.

KNOW YOURSELF

"When you know yourself, you are empowered.
When you accept yourself, you are invincible."

-Tina Lifford

KAREN CAIRES

MONTES CLAROS, BRAZIL

Don't rush. When we are growing up, we face questions like "Who are you? Who are you going to be? What are you going to do?" and the world expect us to have everything figured out at such a young age. You don't have to have the answers for all these questions. Take your time, be yourself. At 13, it's so hard to be patient, but still it is what we need the most to go through every decision and every challenge we encounter.

LORA JOST

CINCINNATI, OHIO

Spend more time finding out what makes you happy, and then make that your life goal, everyday. You are not responsible for anyone's happiness, nor are they responsible for your happiness

NINA NISAR

FRANKFURT, GERMANY

That my body is a temple, just like boys bodies are. Our bodies are sacred. That we each are stunningly beautiful in our very unique expression. And that you are ever evolving, perfectly right where you are right now, and by trusting your ambitions, you are going to get there!

NZINGHA BYRD

CINCINNATI, OHIO

That I have the rest of my life to have sex. There is no need to rush.

JAI WASHINGTON

CINCINNATI, OHIO

I wish someone would have told me that my intuition is a key component of my spiritual compass; please listen to it and trust it. Remember that vulnerability and discernment are important and some of the best resources one can have. Be willing to give yourself double the love you give others. Lastly, know and understand your magic.

PAIGE DICKINSON

FLORIDA

I wish someone would have told me that I was enough when I was 13.

I wish someone would have told me that my scars are a sign of strength and beauty when I was 13.

I wish someone would have told me being sensitive and intuitive is not something to be ashamed of when I was 13.

I wish someone would have told me that it is ok that my strong voice was going to threaten some people, but to never lose it when I was 13.

SARA REITZ

Breasts aren't that important.

SARAH HEIDLER

PORTLAND, OREGON

Your body belongs to you and it is precious. Don't let anybody tell you what you should or should not do with it, don't let anybody cheapen it. Listen to it. It holds a knowledge that is deeper than you realize.

REBECCA HATTARKI

LOS ANGELES, CALIFORNIA

To never believe anything that anybody said about me, even if it was good!

HARRIET KAUFMAN

CINCINNATI, OHIO

When I was 13, I wish someone had told me to listen to my body:

What gives me energy to do more?

What helps me breathe deeply and look around?

What helps me rest and sleep better?

What helps me feel at peace?

What helps me feel like all my different parts fit and work together?

As you take notice of what works for you, find ways do more.

FANCHON SHUR

CINCINNATI, OHIO

I wish somebody would've told me ....when I was 13
that my labia and my vagina were good and that my curiosity about my
body and my skin and my hidden places was natural and beautiful and
right

And that I was beautiful and that my long nose was beautiful and that it
was OK to be afraid when I spoke truth to prejudice. That it was OK to
want to be accepted in the group and that I was wonderful even when I
was being made fun of for being so intellectually sharp.

I wish I had been told that when I was molested by my brother-in-law
and that when it felt good it was not because I was bad, it was because
when I was touched and stimulated on my breasts it's because that's what
my breasts are for—to be sensitive. I wish I had been taught that kind of
touch was good if it came out of my own curiosity with someone my age,
and not someone who could've been my father and who did it without my
permission and I wish someone would've told me that it wasn't up to me to
tell my sister what happened.

I wish I had been told when I was 13 that my menstruation is the proof
that I was a gorgeous wonderful young woman.   *continued*

29

I wish my mother had told me when I was 13 that I was brave to have run away from home at 11 years old and walked 4 1/2 miles to my sisters house.

I wish someone would've told me that dancing is as natural as breathing and my beautiful dancing did not have to be for anybody but for my own pleasure and that was enough.

KNOW YOURSELF

*"Never doubt that you are valuable and powerful and deserving
of every chance and opportunity in the world
to pursue and achieve your own dreams."*

-Hillary Clinton

STEPHANIE LOWRY

CINCINNATI, OHIO

Self-esteem is everything!

KATHRYNE GARDETTE

CINCINNATI, OHIO

To give less than your best, is to sacrifice the gift.

STEPHANIE BORNS

NEW ENGLAND

You are right, and whole and good just as you are. Society and its standards are always shifting and they are not always correct but the core of a young woman has a certain wisdom she can trust and rely on to guide her through to adulthood in safety and dignity.

ROSAURORA ESPINOSA GÓMEZ

MEXICO CITY, MEXICO

That the time to come will be great only if women become stronger and do their best for justice at all levels. This includes our right to be informed about the many changes in our bodies, in our relationships and in our consciousness

AVRIL ORLOFF

VANCOUVER, BRITISH COLUMBIA

I wish someone would have told me that nerdy unpopular girls like me grow up to be the most interesting adults with the most interesting lives, that being "different" was not just OK but really desirable, and that staying true to my convictions (rather than following the pack) was the best way to ensure I lived the life I wanted for myself.

AMBER COOK

ASHEVILLE, NORTH CAROLINA

I wish someone had told me that I was worthy of being taken seriously when I was 13.

YVONNE KELLER

CINCINNATI, OHIO

I wish someone would have told me to spend time every day to figure out my own opinion on something and value it

DONNA ALVARADO

That they loved me.

CARYN FLOWERS

INDIANAPOLIS, INDIANA

I was already whole.

CARESSE CRANWELL

TUGUN, AUSTRALIA

When I was 13 I wish someone would have told me I was as good as any boy! So I could be my own unique person without having to compete or resent the boys having the center ground all the time! I could stand proud in myself!

MELISSA WILLIAMS

NEW YORK, NEW YORK

When I was 13 I wish someone would have told me that my value is not determined by my academic success or work productivity. At 36 I have to still work on the repercussions of this, namely workaholism and perfectionism.

STEPHANIE WHITE ALDRIDGE

PARDEEVILLE, WISCONSIN

Speak up...don't hide or lie when you have troubles or worries. Your friends will listen and they care. This message I have told my girls—that there is strength untouched in us all...tap into it

MARY ALICE ARTHUR

DENMARK

When I was young and in primary school, I felt like I was capable and respected—a leader. When I turned 13, that all seemed to change, suddenly the rules were different. I wish someone would have told me back then that "this too will pass" and that it would take time for me to grow into myself and discover my own beauty and talent. I wish I'd known that every person has their own unique gifts and timing and that part of growing up is growing enough patience, resilience and insight to know your time and when it comes, to leap! Little sister, your time is coming!

BARBARA MCAFEE

MINNEAPOLIS, MINNESOTA

It's okay to be weird, to not fit in.
Weird is just another name for "interesting."
The bullies who are making your daily life misery now
are actually miserable themselves.
Their misery is likely to continue; yours is not.

Your parents don't have everything you need to grow up to be who you
are meant to be.
Keep a lookout for other adults who see and appreciate you.
Let them in.

The hard times now are giving you great gifts that will bloom later on.
Keep loving what you love.
Keep laughing at the craziness.
Stay close to the friends who build you up.
Trust the greater pattern of your life.
You are headed to an amazing life, young one.
Hang in there....

BE KIND

"Before you know kindness as the deepest thing inside,
you must know sorrow as the other deepest thing.
You must wake up with sorrow. You must speak to it till your voice catches
the thread of all sorrows and you see the size of the cloth. Then it is only
kindness that makes sense anymore,
only kindness that ties your shoes and sends you out into the day to gaze at
bread, only kindness that raises its head from the crowd of the world to say
It is I you have been looking for, and then goes with you everywhere like a
shadow or a friend."

-Naomi Shihab Nye

LORENA MORATA RUIZ

YONKERS, NEW YORK

I wish someone would have told me not to be too hard on myself.

NADA HOSNI

MOOSE JAW, SASKATCHEWAN

I wish someone would have told me how important it is to love yourself
and your body when I was 13.

SUE ELLIOTT

ALISO VIEJO, CALIFORNIA

I wish someone would have told me that how I feel about myself changes everything (including how other people see me) when I was 13.

AKOSUA FAVORS

CINCINNATI, OHIO

Your attitude makes you beautiful not your outward appearance!

NICOLE SIMONE ALEXANDER

MELBOURNE, AUSTRALIA

I wish someone had told me that it's ok to be gentle on myself, that I am lovable just as I am. That I don't need to be perfect, rather aim for 80% and celebrate the messiness of being human - when I was 13.

MONICA PILEGGI

MIAMI, FLORIDA

I wish someone would have told me about the importance of empathy and recognizing others when I was 13. In every situation you face in life there are two things that you have to look at to get the best results. Sometimes it is important to contol the situation, or to insist your point of view be considered when you face opposing points of view and nobody wants to give in. But it is also important to have a more peaceful and rewarding life. It is incredible that when you put yourself in the shoes of others and really think about why the other person is behaving in a certain way, you get a totally different perspective. You realize that nothing is that difficult, or you see that the problem just vanishes.

I wish someone would have told me "the real meaning of happiness in life" when I was 13, so we could have spread the word and seen how people could have enjoyed their lives better by just doing what they really loved and not what the society expected from them. To be happy is just to be the real you.

JULIANE BELISLE

CINCINNATI, OHIO

That everybody was feeling just as awkward and uncomfortable as I was.

One of the most powerful things that was actually said to me was "you are a nice person and you are loveable." My father told me this when I was wading through some peer conflict and attempting to set boundaries. I'm sure part of the power was that this came from my father. And part of the power was because he said it at the exact moment I was most unsure of this.

I wish I would have understood or known that my peers were simply trying on the hats of their families, as was I. We were all just trying to make sense of ourselves in the context of where we were from. We had no idea who we were at that time. This may have helped me not be so wounded as gender roles and sexuality were expressed and tested.

I watch my daughter as an awareness of feminism and social justice dawns within her. Meanwhile the boys she has played with and shared friendship with since preschool now mock or tease her for asking questions like "What are you afraid would happen if a woman were president? Why are you afraid of a woman being in charge?" She is wounded, because their antics are not just a mocking of an idea but a violation of friendship. These boys whom I have known since they were 3 years old are not bad. They have no idea of the violation they have committed. They are trying on hats. Maybe the hats of their fathers. Maybe they are trying on a hat in direct opposition to their family. They are trying to see what fits. As is she. But it feels so raw when you're 13. I imagine it feels raw for them too.

CARPE DIEM

"Show up in every single moment like you're meant to be there."

-Marie Forleo

HEBATALLA GAMAL DESOUKY

MOOSE JAW, SASKATCHEWAN

That time passes very fast, and I needed to enjoy every moment that I had with my mom, dad and sisters. No one knows where life will be taking you to.

JUDITH STEMERDINK-HERRET

VIENNA, AUSTRIA

I wish someone would have told me … how fast life passes by. Every minute is so precious because you have the freedom and responsibility of choice in life. Dare to do things that you feel are important for you and the world. Others cannot decide for you. You have your life in your hands. Breath, feel the present moment, relax … when I was 13.

TAY MINEER

CINCINNATI, OHIO

Study music, learn to sing and learn to make music with others.

COURTNEY BRYAN-CARON

MALIBU, CALIFORNIA

To savor each moment of my temporal life and the people who pass through it.

NANCY M. LAIRD

CINCINNATI, OHIO

That everything in the world was possible for me to try. No limits. Nothing—money, education, anything. Desire and passion will take us to amazing places.

SABRINA HOLLOWAY

CLEVELAND, OHIO

That it's okay to dream.

QUANITA ROBERSON

CINCINNATI, OHIO

I wish someone would have told me that life is messy and that I was here to make noise, screw up, fart in public, dance wild and crazy while everyone was looking, and cry the ugly cry at least once a day. I wish someone would have told me that there was something that I knew and could do that no one else did and my job was to discover that thing during my lifetime. I wish someone would have told me that I was worth it, and it didn't matter what the *it* was. I wish someone would have told me that not only was I loved and lovable but I was love itself.

AMY TUTTLE

CINCINNATI, OHIO

Go boldly into the unknown. It is OK to not yet know exactly where you are headed and who you are becoming. Develop a sense of delicious curiosity around the stories that most inspire you. Be confident in the process of allowing an authentic discovery of your deepest gifts and long-ings. Listen to the subtle directions that your gut invites you to explore. Befriend mystery. Say yes to the adventures that life unfolds! Over time, the colorful threads that you follow will weave themselves together into a vibrant harmony of identity and purpose. The weaving of your divine, unique story in the world is a life-long process, never quite complete, always revealing more and more beauty. Breathe, love, pray, savor.

I AM WORTHY

"I am strong. I am beautiful. I am enough."
-Vanessa Pawlowski

JANA FREIBERGER

LONGVIEW, WASHINGTON

To have a plan for saying no and standing up for myself BEFORE the boys began pressuring me.

JUDITH-KATE FRIEDMAN

PORT TOWNSEND, WASHINGTON

When I was 13 I wish someone would have told me—We all make mistakes and no one is perfect no matter what anyone might tell you. You are beautiful and worthy!!! Already! No need to prove this to anyone :) Don't let anyone shame you.

People of all kinds and ages will say all sorts of things about you as if they are true. Trust your inner sense of what to believe. You know what's true deep inside. Many positive things people say may ring true as compliments. Let them in.

However, when someone comes at you with negatives or "shoulds" or "helpful suggestions" that aren't really helpful, these are often based on that person's own challenges. Say thank you and just shine them on. If they rattle you, turn to a trusted elder or mentor to get their view, and let yours tears and fears out. You're already a brilliant, intelligent, strong, soulful, caring, wonderful being with great heart, body, mind, creative talents and possibilities. You always were and you always will be.

Pay attention to what makes you truly feel good and clear and hang around with the people with whom and the situations where you feel most powerful, relaxed and like you can be your real self. Life is supposed to be both serious AND fun! (Go for both!)

Not everyone will appreciate you and it's never worth chasing anyone even if it seems like it is. Rather: be what you love and allow who you are to take its time. Trees take a while to root and grow. Some flowers take some years before they're booming with blooming. Lots more will be revealed. Take your time. In the end of any journey, honesty, patience and kindness matter more than racing or speeding across a finish line. There are always choices and almost always second (and third and fourth) chances.

Don't worry if things get confusing. They just are that way, often. We all learn over time. Over our whole lifetimes. At thirteen you're at a thresh-old of your growing up life. It's okay to be a beginner and to ask questions. It's okay to not know.
There's a difference between complicated and complex. Life IS complex! You and everyone and everything have many, many layers. This is good.

Explore what you love. Find allies among peers, mentors and the living world of Nature. Turn to them when ever you feel the need - even if it's simply for connection.

If you ever feel like you're not loving yourself or not being well loved, ask them about this. Get more than one opinion. There are thousands of gates to the palace of wisdom.

PAMELA RICHIE ENZ

MINNEAPOLIS, MINNESOTA

I wish someone would have told me I was really smart (not just pretty) when I was 13.

WE NEED EACH OTHER

"Your work is to let love all the way in and to offer love all the way out."

-Christina Baldwin

YUKO WATANABE

KONOSU, SAITAMA, JAPAN

When I was 13 I wish someone would have told me I will always be beside you, even when something bad happen.

ROZY PARK

I wish someone would have told me how little I should care what the "popular kids" were doing, and instead to enjoy my friends and relationships, and to value people for who they actually were, regardless of whether they were "popular." All that stuff doesn't matter, and you all grow up to be real people with both happiness and challenges.

KATHY JOURDAIN

BEDFORD, NOVA SCOTIA

When I was 13, I wish someone would have told me I was not "alone" in the world, that I would find my soul pods and that the gifts I had were real, not imaginary. I wish someone would have told me about soul journeys and supported me in finding my way - because there is beauty, grace and wisdom in abundance when we know where and how to look.

ANN LINNEA

WHIDBEY ISLAND, WASHINGTON

I wish someone would have told me that I could find ways to pursue my deep love of nature as part of a profession. When I was 13 (1962), I looked around and could see very, very few role models for athletic, outdoor women. And I had no exposure to environmental issues until I went to college. There Dr. Lois Tiffany opened the world of nature, science, and passionate care for all living things to me. Look for your mentors. We are waiting for you.

LAUREN CASAMASSIMA

BROOKLYN, NEW YORK

The value of girlfriends. They are your chosen family. Your sisters, healers, teachers, fan club, motivation and inspiration. Girlfriends will have your back, hold space for you, provide a shoulder to cry on and hold that much needed mirror up to you when you're being stubborn, deflecting, projecting or avoiding. They will do this with love to challenge you and then they will hold you through the breakdown/breakthrough. They will walk through the darkness by your side and confront the shadows with their moonlight.

I AM POWER-FILLED

"She remembered who she was and the game changed."

-Lalah Deliah

MEGHAN CLARKE

I wish someone would have told me when I was 13 that I was powerful beyond measure. That my ability to feel, empathize and understand the emotions, expressed and unexpressed, of those around me was a gift to be honored not hidden. That my intuition was an unearned gift from the creator to be shared with those around me, not to be squelched or otherwise silenced, as 'what could I possibly know as a 13 year old?' I wish that someone had told me to speak up even if my voice cracked and it meant standing up to the people I was supposed to honor. I wish that someone would have told me that all of the tribulations I was experiencing were not mine to bear alone but instead were to be shared with others. That these very experiences would define who I am and make me all the stronger for it. That both the pain and joy were equal parts of the equation. That the lessons that I would take from these experiences and from those around me would one day turn into the wisdom that is core to my being. I wish that someone would have told me early on to love and honor my whole self: the snort when I laugh, the sassiness, the fire wand, the compassion, the anger and the fierce, vulnerable little girl who resides within me.

PAIGE WALKER

SYDNEY, AUSTRALIA

"You are what you think. So just think big, believe big, act big, work big, give big, forgive big, laugh big, love big and live big."
—Andrew Carnegie

THIES MORATA

CINCINNATI, OHIO

I wish some one would have told me that while I cannot control events or people I can control my reaction.

ZOE MCGINN

I wish someone would have told me when I was 13 that if I projected confidence, dumb boys would have cowered in my shadow instead of making fun of me. That self-assured ambition and love for myself would draw the perfect people to me.

DARSHEEL KAUR

HARRISONBURG, VIRGINIA

I wish someone would have told me I had the power to affect my feelings
and experiences when I was 13..

KATIE SPACEK

OAKLAND, CALIFORNIA

When I was 13, I wish someone would have told me that no matter what happens, you ALWAYS have a safe place in feeling yourself breathe, and a superpower in watching your own thoughts. Every breath is different, but you don't realize it unless you ride each wave beginning to end with all your focus. And thoughts are never "good" or "bad" because you cannot control them. You can watch them, though, and this gives you power and courage to do the best you can do

OSUNLADE DAPHNE EDWARDS-EMI

DALLAS, TEXAS

That I was powerful beyond measure

YOU ARE NOT
RESPONSIBLE FOR OTHERS

"You can't save a damsel if she loves her distress."

-anonymous

RITA SINORITA FIERRO

PHILADELPHIA, PENNSYLVANIA

You are not your parent's source of life. It is not your job to make them happy or heal their pain. It is your job to heal your pain, and ONLY your pain. Let silence teach you where the pain is in your body and let it flow, then let it go. Then make space every day for things that bring you joy. Joy will show you the way for healing. And one day, one day, fitting in won't matter anymore. Actually, everything that makes you NOT fit in, that you feel deeply, that you're smart, that you're beautiful, will make you a cool, attractive, interesting, and captivating woman. There's NOTH-ING wrong with you for not fitting in. It's just the way life goes...and it's an adventure!"

ELAINE JONES HANSEN

I wish I had known that even the popular kids were feeling insecure. At my 20year high school class reunion, I learned that during high school, the popular kids had the same anxieties about being accepted as I did. I had thought they were so together and had it all. Back then, I wish I had known that I didn't have to bend myself into a pretzel so everyone would like me. Being my authentic self is enough without bending to other people's expectations. I am enough. You are enough.

I wish I had known to take care of myself first and use the power of my "No". It has taken me a long time to learn that lesson. Growing up, I was taught I wasn't allowed to say "No". My mother was wrong to teach me that.

It sounds strange now to say it, but I thought my "No" had the power to hurt someone's feelings. And, nice girls don't hurt other people's feel-ings. Because I never said no, it left no time or space for me to do what I wanted to do. It also meant that instead of saying no, I would quietly remove myself from the situation. A boy made a pass at me my freshman year in college. Instead of telling him no, I refused his calls and avoided him. In hindsight, it would have been more honest to tell him why I didn't want to see him again.

Discovering my "No" and my personal agency has changed my life. In all circumstances, I get to choose who I allow into my life, how I show up in the world, how engaged I want to be. I had to learn the only person I was responsible for is myself. My responsibility to others is to honor my commitments.

TIMI SINGLEY

COLUMBUS, OHIO

I wish someone would have told me that it was ok to cry, because I cry anyway. I wish that someone would have told me that my intuition is to be trusted and that second guessing myself is a waste of time. I wish someone would have told me that the broken heart I would feel from friends not accepting me is really their trauma and insecurity and not mine and that my capacity to forgive that hurt is the path to healing my broken heart. I wish someone would have told me that loving others so deeply is the way that the Divine shows up in me, is me, and that my fear was only me loving myself too. I wish someone would have told me that my greatest gift was just me and I am always enough.

ABOUT THIS BOOK

This is the second book in the Soul Growing series. The first one was for boys so it was natural to follow it up with a book for girls because I have a daughter and because I know so many
strong women. I often tell my own daughter to look for her community mamas. There are women in the world that have gifts for her that I'm not capable of giving her. I hope that this book, these women will be her guides as she finds her way in the world. I know they have been mine and will continue to be as I find my way.

QUANITA ROBERSON, MA

Quanita Roberson (www.nzuzu.com) is a personal and professional development facilitator dedicated to addressing embedded trauma through healing workshops, retreats, and rituals. Quanita is an international spiritual teacher, speaker, author, and life coach. She holds a master's degree in Organizational Management and Development with a concentration in Integral Theory. She holds a certification in Embodying Creative Leadership through Growth in Motion and is a wisdom keeper of ancient indigenous wisdom from the Dagara Tribe of Burkina Faso, West Africa. As a water spirit, she brings the gifts of forgiveness and reconciliation — serving as a peacemaker and bridge builder to communities around the world. She is a results oriented individual with experience in convening community conversations, healing internal and external conflict, and blending ancient wisdom with contemporary practices.